# Politics 101

## The Ins & Outs of U.S. Politics

Daniel A. Garcia

# Dedication

This is dedicated to all staffers working in our U.S. Congress. Thank you for your hard work.


Go Get 'EM!

# How To Use

<u>This journal is made up of the following:</u>

- Check list: To check off questions. Gives a visual of progress made, in this particular journal.
- Note section: To make note of activity.

<u>Divided into four (4) sections:</u>

- The three branches -  executive, legislative, and judicial branches of government.
- Finding your ideal political party.
- Taking action – getting involved.
- Paying it forward.

# The Three Branches

In this section – the focus is on the three branches of government. Which are the executive, legislative, and judicial branches of our U.S. government. It's always good – to have some general knowledge about each. This is how our democracy functions – with checks and balances. Making sure each branch is not over powering another.

These same branches, apply to state and local governments. For example, in a city, the executive branch would be the mayor, legislative branch – the city council, and judicial branch the city/county court judge.

For this journal – we will focus on the federal/national level positions.

# Executive Branch – The President of the United States

Every four years – U.S. citizens over the age of 18 have the greatest privilege, civil duty, and freedom – which is to vote.

We cast our vote for our choice of candidate – for President. The President is the commander and chief. POTUS can pass bills/sign executive orders that affect our foreign policy, economy, healthcare, etc. A U.S. President is able to serve a maximum of two (2) terms of four (4) years. Totaling in eight (8) years. Some have only served one term of 4 years.  President Franklin D. Roosevelt (FDR) was the only POTUS to serve 3 terms – and began a fourth. Nearly two decades serving as President.

Use the following section – to list your favorite President(s). And their main focus/agenda.

President _________________________________ Terms:_______

❏ Did you vote for this President, as a candidate?
Were you glad you voted for this President?

___________________________________________

___________________________________________

___________________________________________

___________________________________________

___________________________________________

❏ What was this President's party? Is he
Republican, Democrat, Independent, or another
party?

___________________________________________

___________________________________________

___________________________________________

___________________________________________

❏ What was the focus/agenda of this President? Do
you believe he delivered on his promises?

___________________________________________

___________________________________________

___________________________________________

___________________________________________

❏ Do you feel this leader of the free world – made
the best of his term(s) for the betterment of the
U.S.?

___________________________________________

___________________________________________

___________________________________________

___________________________________________

President ________________________________ Terms:______

❑ Did you vote for this President, as a candidate?
  Were you glad you voted for this President?

_______________________________________________

_______________________________________________

_______________________________________________

_______________________________________________

_______________________________________________

❑ What was this President's party? Is he
  Republican, Democrat, Independent, or another
  party?

_______________________________________________

_______________________________________________

_______________________________________________

_______________________________________________

❑ What was the focus/agenda of this President? Do
  you believe he delivered on his promises?

_______________________________________________

_______________________________________________

_______________________________________________

_______________________________________________

_______________________________________________

❑ Do you feel this leader of the free world – made
  the best of his term(s) for the betterment of the
  U.S.?

_______________________________________________

_______________________________________________

_______________________________________________

_______________________________________________

President _________________________________ Terms:_______

❑ Did you vote for this President, as a candidate? Were you glad you voted for this President?

_______________________________________

_______________________________________

_______________________________________

_______________________________________

_______________________________________

❑ What was this President's party? Is he Republican, Democrat, Independent, or another party?

_______________________________________

_______________________________________

_______________________________________

_______________________________________

_______________________________________

❑ What was the focus/agenda of this President? Do you believe he delivered on his promises?

_______________________________________

_______________________________________

_______________________________________

_______________________________________

❑ Do you feel this leader of the free world – made the best of his term(s) for the betterment of the U.S.?

_______________________________________

_______________________________________

_______________________________________

_______________________________________

President _________________________________ Terms: _______

❑ Did you vote for this President, as a candidate? Were you glad you voted for this President?

_______________________________________________

_______________________________________________

_______________________________________________

_______________________________________________

❑ What was this President's party? Is he Republican, Democrat, Independent, or another party?

_______________________________________________

_______________________________________________

_______________________________________________

_______________________________________________

❑ What was the focus/agenda of this President? Do you believe he delivered on his promises?

_______________________________________________

_______________________________________________

_______________________________________________

_______________________________________________

❑ Do you feel this leader of the free world – made the best of his term(s) for the betterment of the U.S.?

_______________________________________________

_______________________________________________

_______________________________________________

_______________________________________________

President _________________________________ Terms:________

❑ Did you vote for this President, as a candidate? Were you glad you voted for this President?

_______________________________________

_______________________________________

_______________________________________

_______________________________________

_______________________________________

❑ What was this President's party? Is he Republican, Democrat, Independent, or another party?

_______________________________________

_______________________________________

_______________________________________

_______________________________________

❑ What was the focus/agenda of this President? Do you believe he delivered on his promises?

_______________________________________

_______________________________________

_______________________________________

_______________________________________

_______________________________________

❑ Do you feel this leader of the free world – made the best of his term(s) for the betterment of the U.S.?

_______________________________________

_______________________________________

_______________________________________

_______________________________________

President _______________________________Terms:______

❑ Did you vote for this President, as a candidate?
  Were you glad you voted for this President?

______________________________________________

______________________________________________

______________________________________________

______________________________________________

______________________________________________

❑ What was this President's party? Is he
  Republican, Democrat, Independent, or another
  party?

______________________________________________

______________________________________________

______________________________________________

______________________________________________

❑ What was the focus/agenda of this President? Do
  you believe he delivered on his promises?

______________________________________________

______________________________________________

______________________________________________

______________________________________________

______________________________________________

❑ Do you feel this leader of the free world – made
  the best of his term(s) for the betterment of the
  U.S.?

______________________________________________

______________________________________________

______________________________________________

______________________________________________

# Legislative Branch – Congress

Congress is made up of the U.S. Senate and U.S. House of Representatives. Both make up Capital Hill.

Each State has two Senators on their behalf in Washington, D.C. A total of 100 Senators in the U.S. Senate. Each Sen. may serve an unlimited number of six-year terms.

The House of Reps – Is based upon the population (divided into districts) of each state. But, each state is entitled to at least one representative. So, the number varies – state to state. Each Rep. may serve an unlimited number of two-year terms.

Both are responsible for passing legislation – laws of the land, for the people and serve different purposes; depending on a senator/representative's agenda.

Use the following pages, to list leaders of the Senate and House. Along with your state's U.S. Senators and Representatives.

# U.S. Senate Leadership – The Vice-President

The Vice-President of the U.S. is selected by a presidential candidate. The two then campaign, with their efforts targeted at being elected.

After the President, the VP is the next person in line – should anything happen to the President; the VP is then sworn in as the President.

In the Senate – the Vice-President – is the President of the Senate and oversees the Senate's operations and work carried on the Senate floor. When absent, the President Pro Tempore, a high-ranking Senator of the majority party, resides over.

The VP can only vote on a bill, when needed to break a tie – his position carries substantial weight in the Senate.

Vice-President _________________ Term(s): _____

❑ Where is this VP from? What is the result of the presidential election, how did the campaign do?

____________________________________________

____________________________________________

____________________________________________

____________________________________________

❑ What party does this VP belong to? Republican, Democrat, Independent, or another party?

____________________________________________

____________________________________________

____________________________________________

____________________________________________

____________________________________________

❑ How is this Vice-President's performance, in the Senate? How many ties, has he had to break?

____________________________________________

____________________________________________

____________________________________________

____________________________________________

❑ Does this VP work well - alongside the President? Do they make a good team?

____________________________________________

____________________________________________

____________________________________________

Vice-President________________ Term(s):_____

❑ Where is this VP from? What is the result of the presidential election, how did the campaign do?

___________________________________________

___________________________________________

___________________________________________

___________________________________________

❑ What party does this VP belong to? Republican, Democrat, Independent, or another party?

___________________________________________

___________________________________________

___________________________________________

___________________________________________

❑ How is this Vice-President's performance, in the Senate? How many ties, has he had to break?

___________________________________________

___________________________________________

___________________________________________

___________________________________________

❑ Does this VP work well - alongside the President? Do they make a good team?

___________________________________________

___________________________________________

___________________________________________

___________________________________________

Vice-President ________________________ Term(s): ______

❑ Where is this VP from? What is the result of the
   presidential election, how did the campaign do?

_______________________________________________

_______________________________________________

_______________________________________________

_______________________________________________

❑ What party does this VP belong to? Republican,
   Democrat, Independent, or another party?

_______________________________________________

_______________________________________________

_______________________________________________

_______________________________________________

❑ How is this Vice-President's performance, in the
   Senate? How many ties, has he had to break?

_______________________________________________

_______________________________________________

_______________________________________________

_______________________________________________

❑ Does this VP work well - alongside the President? Do
   they make a good team?

_______________________________________________

_______________________________________________

_______________________________________________

_______________________________________________

Vice-President __________________________ Term(s):______

❑ Where is this VP from? What is the result of the presidential election, how did the campaign do?

_______________________________________________

_______________________________________________

_______________________________________________

_______________________________________________

_______________________________________________

❑ What party does this VP belong to? Republican, Democrat, Independent, or another party?

_______________________________________________

_______________________________________________

_______________________________________________

_______________________________________________

_______________________________________________

❑ How is this Vice-President's performance, in the Senate? How many ties, has he had to break?

_______________________________________________

_______________________________________________

_______________________________________________

_______________________________________________

_______________________________________________

❑ Does this VP work well - alongside the President? Do they make a good team?

_______________________________________________

_______________________________________________

_______________________________________________

_______________________________________________

Vice-President _______________________ Term(s):________

❏ Where is this VP from? What is the result of the presidential election, how did the campaign do?

_________________________________________

_________________________________________

_________________________________________

_________________________________________

_________________________________________

❏ What party does this VP belong to? Republican, Democrat, Independent, or another party?

_________________________________________

_________________________________________

_________________________________________

_________________________________________

_________________________________________

❏ How is this Vice-President's performance, in the Senate? How many ties, has he had to break?

_________________________________________

_________________________________________

_________________________________________

_________________________________________

❏ Does this VP work well - alongside the President? Do they make a good team?

_________________________________________

_________________________________________

_________________________________________

_________________________________________

U.S. Senator______________________Term(s):______

❑ Where is this Senator from, which State? What is the result of his/her election, how did the campaign do?

_______________________________________________

_______________________________________________

_______________________________________________

_______________________________________________

_______________________________________________

❑ What party does this Senator belong to? Republican, Democrat, Independent, or another party?

_______________________________________________

_______________________________________________

_______________________________________________

_______________________________________________

_______________________________________________

❑ What is the focus/agenda of this Sen.? Have they delivered on their promises?

_______________________________________________

_______________________________________________

_______________________________________________

_______________________________________________

_______________________________________________

❑ Do you believe, this official listens to his/her constituents? Have they ran in a presidential race?

_______________________________________________

_______________________________________________

_______________________________________________

U.S. Senator__________________________Term(s):______

❑ Where is this Senator from, which State? What is the
result of his/her election, how did the campaign do?

_______________________________________________

_______________________________________________

_______________________________________________

_______________________________________________

❑ What party does this Senator belong to? Republican,
Democrat, Independent, or another party?

_______________________________________________

_______________________________________________

_______________________________________________

_______________________________________________

❑ What is the focus/agenda of this Sen.? Have they
delivered on their promises?

_______________________________________________

_______________________________________________

_______________________________________________

_______________________________________________

❑ Do you believe, this official listens to his/her
constituents? Have they ran in a presidential race?

_______________________________________________

_______________________________________________

_______________________________________________

_______________________________________________

U.S. Senator_________________________Term(s):______

❑ Where is this Senator from, which State? What is the
  result of his/her election, how did the campaign do?

___________________________________________________

___________________________________________________

___________________________________________________

___________________________________________________

___________________________________________________

❑ What party does this Senator belong to? Republican,
  Democrat, Independent, or another party?

___________________________________________________

___________________________________________________

___________________________________________________

___________________________________________________

___________________________________________________

❑ What is the focus/agenda of this Sen.? Have they
  delivered on their promises?

___________________________________________________

___________________________________________________

___________________________________________________

___________________________________________________

___________________________________________________

❑ Do you believe, this official listens to his/her
  constituents? Have they ran in a presidential race?

___________________________________________________

___________________________________________________

___________________________________________________

___________________________________________________

U.S. Senator______________________________Term(s):________

❑ Where is this Senator from, which State? What is the result of his/her election, how did the campaign do?

_______________________________________________

_______________________________________________

_______________________________________________

_______________________________________________

_______________________________________________

❑ What party does this Senator belong to? Republican, Democrat, Independent, or another party?

_______________________________________________

_______________________________________________

_______________________________________________

_______________________________________________

_______________________________________________

❑ What is the focus/agenda of this Sen.? Have they delivered on their promises?

_______________________________________________

_______________________________________________

_______________________________________________

_______________________________________________

_______________________________________________

❑ Do you believe, this official listens to his/her constituents? Have they ran in a presidential race?

_______________________________________________

_______________________________________________

_______________________________________________

_______________________________________________

## U.S. Senator_______________________Term(s):______

❑ Where is this Senator from, which State? What is the result of his/her election, how did the campaign do?

_______________________________________________
_______________________________________________
_______________________________________________
_______________________________________________
_______________________________________________

❑ What party does this Senator belong to? Republican, Democrat, Independent, or another party?

_______________________________________________
_______________________________________________
_______________________________________________
_______________________________________________
_______________________________________________

❑ What is the focus/agenda of this Sen.? Have they delivered on their promises?

_______________________________________________
_______________________________________________
_______________________________________________
_______________________________________________
_______________________________________________

❑ Do you believe, this official listens to his/her constituents? Have they ran in a presidential race?

_______________________________________________
_______________________________________________
_______________________________________________
_______________________________________________

# U.S. House of Representatives' Leadership – The Speaker of the House

The Speaker of the House of U.S. Reps. is the official officer and political leader of the House of Representatives. The House votes to elect a new speaker – with every new Congress or if the incumbent dies, resigns, or is removed from the position.

The Speaker is usually head of the majority party in the House. He or She is able to vote and even debate in the proceedings of the House. With many tasks, an important one includes, the swearing in of new Representatives, newly elected to their seat.

In the line succession, as follows, it's The Vice-President, Speaker of the House, President Pro Tempore. Making the Speaker second in line to the Presidency.

House Speaker________________________ Term(s): ______

❑ Where is this Speaker from? Have they served as a
Representative, before?

______________________________________________

______________________________________________

______________________________________________

______________________________________________

______________________________________________

❑ What party does this Speaker belong to? Republican
Democrat, Independent, or another party?

______________________________________________

______________________________________________

______________________________________________

______________________________________________

______________________________________________

❑ When voting for your state's Reps., do you hope for
your party, to gain the House majority?

______________________________________________

______________________________________________

______________________________________________

______________________________________________

______________________________________________

❑ Does this Speaker preside, fairly? How is the working
relationship, with the President and Vice-President?

______________________________________________

______________________________________________

______________________________________________

______________________________________________

House Speaker_______________________ Term(s):______

❑ Where is this Speaker from? Have they served as a
Representative, before?

_______________________________________________

_______________________________________________

_______________________________________________

_______________________________________________

_______________________________________________

❑ What party does this Speaker belong to? Republican,
Democrat, Independent, or another party?

_______________________________________________

_______________________________________________

_______________________________________________

_______________________________________________

_______________________________________________

❑ When voting for your state's Reps., do you hope for
your party, to gain the House majority?

_______________________________________________

_______________________________________________

_______________________________________________

_______________________________________________

❑ Does this Speaker preside, fairly? How is the working
relationship, with the President and Vice-President?

_______________________________________________

_______________________________________________

_______________________________________________

House Speaker_____________________ Term(s):______

❑ Where is this Speaker from? Have they served as a
   Representative, before?

______________________________________________

______________________________________________

______________________________________________

______________________________________________

______________________________________________

❑ What party does this Speaker belong to? Republican,
   Democrat, Independent, or another party?

______________________________________________

______________________________________________

______________________________________________

______________________________________________

______________________________________________

❑ When voting for your state's Reps., do you hope for
   your party, to gain the House majority?

______________________________________________

______________________________________________

______________________________________________

______________________________________________

______________________________________________

❑ Does this Speaker preside, fairly? How is the working
   relationship, with the President and Vice-President?

______________________________________________

______________________________________________

______________________________________________

______________________________________________

House Speaker_________________ Term(s):_______

❑ Where is this Speaker from? Have they served as a
Representative, before?

_______________________________________________

_______________________________________________

_______________________________________________

_______________________________________________

_______________________________________________

❑ What party does this Speaker belong to? Republican,
Democrat, Independent, or another party?

_______________________________________________

_______________________________________________

_______________________________________________

_______________________________________________

_______________________________________________

❑ When voting for your state's Reps., do you hope for
your party, to gain the House majority?

_______________________________________________

_______________________________________________

_______________________________________________

_______________________________________________

❑ Does this Speaker preside, fairly? How is the working
relationship, with the President and Vice-President?

_______________________________________________

_______________________________________________

_______________________________________________

_______________________________________________

## House Speaker_______________________ Term(s):______

❑ Where is this Speaker from? Have they served as a Representative, before?

_______________________________________________

_______________________________________________

_______________________________________________

_______________________________________________

❑ What party does this Speaker belong to? Republican, Democrat, Independent, or another party?

_______________________________________________

_______________________________________________

_______________________________________________

_______________________________________________

❑ When voting for your state's Reps., do you hope for your party, to gain the House majority?

_______________________________________________

_______________________________________________

_______________________________________________

_______________________________________________

❑ Does this Speaker preside, fairly? How is the working relationship, with the President and Vice-President?

_______________________________________________

_______________________________________________

_______________________________________________

U.S. Rep.__________________________ Term(s):______

❑ Where is this Representative from, which State?
What were the results of his/her election?

_______________________________________________

_______________________________________________

_______________________________________________

_______________________________________________

_______________________________________________

❑ What party does this Rep. belong to? Republican,
Democrat, Independent, or another party?

_______________________________________________

_______________________________________________

_______________________________________________

_______________________________________________

_______________________________________________

❑ What is the focus/agenda of this Rep.? Have they
delivered on their promises?

_______________________________________________

_______________________________________________

_______________________________________________

_______________________________________________

❑ Do you believe, this official listens to his/her
constituents? Have they ran in a presidential race?

_______________________________________________

_______________________________________________

_______________________________________________

U.S. Rep._________________________ Term(s):______

❑ Where is this Representative from, which State? What were the results of his/her election?

_______________________________________________

_______________________________________________

_______________________________________________

_______________________________________________

_______________________________________________

❑ What party does this Rep. belong to? Republican, Democrat, Independent, or another party?

_______________________________________________

_______________________________________________

_______________________________________________

_______________________________________________

_______________________________________________

❑ What is the focus/agenda of this Rep.? Have they delivered on their promises?

_______________________________________________

_______________________________________________

_______________________________________________

_______________________________________________

_______________________________________________

❑ Do you believe, this official listens to his/her constituents? Have they ran in a presidential race?

_______________________________________________

_______________________________________________

_______________________________________________

_______________________________________________

## U.S. Rep._______________________ Term(s):______

❑ Where is this Representative from, which State?
What were the results of his/her election?

_______________________________________

_______________________________________

_______________________________________

_______________________________________

❑ What party does this Rep. belong to? Republican,
Democrat, Independent, or another party?

_______________________________________

_______________________________________

_______________________________________

_______________________________________

❑ What is the focus/agenda of this Rep.? Have they
delivered on their promises?

_______________________________________

_______________________________________

_______________________________________

_______________________________________

❑ Do you believe, this official listens to his/her
constituents? Have they ran in a presidential race?

_______________________________________

_______________________________________

_______________________________________

_______________________________________

U.S. Rep._________________________Term(s):______

❑ Where is this Representative from, which State?
   What were the results of his/her election?

_______________________________________________

_______________________________________________

_______________________________________________

_______________________________________________

_______________________________________________

❑ What party does this Rep. belong to? Republican,
   Democrat, Independent, or another party?

_______________________________________________

_______________________________________________

_______________________________________________

_______________________________________________

_______________________________________________

❑ What is the focus/agenda of this Rep.? Have they
   delivered on their promises?

_______________________________________________

_______________________________________________

_______________________________________________

_______________________________________________

_______________________________________________

❑ Do you believe, this official listens to his/her
   constituents? Have they ran in a presidential race?

_______________________________________________

_______________________________________________

_______________________________________________

_______________________________________________

U.S. Rep._______________________________Term(s):_______

❑ Where is this Representative from, which State?
What were the results of his/her election?

_______________________________________________

_______________________________________________

_______________________________________________

_______________________________________________

_______________________________________________

❑ What party does this Rep. belong to? Republican,
Democrat, Independent, or another party?

_______________________________________________

_______________________________________________

_______________________________________________

_______________________________________________

_______________________________________________

❑ What is the focus/agenda of this Rep.? Have they
delivered on their promises?

_______________________________________________

_______________________________________________

_______________________________________________

_______________________________________________

_______________________________________________

❑ Do you believe, this official listens to his/her
constituents? Have they ran in a presidential race?

_______________________________________________

_______________________________________________

_______________________________________________

# Judicial Branch – The Supreme Court

The supreme court, is the highest court in the U.S. which is made up of nine (9) supreme court justices. A justice candidate is nominated by the President – and confirmed by the U.S. Senate.

Each member can serve for life – or until they retire. The justices can serve with different presidents.

The supreme court handles federal cases and makes critical decisions. These decisions have an impact that affects everyone. Some local and state cases get passed up to the Supreme Court, when they aren't solved in their local or state trial.

The following section – you can use for each supreme court member; either current or past.

# U.S. Justice  ______________________

❑ What President nominated this Justice? How many Presidents, have they served under?

________________________________________

________________________________________

________________________________________

________________________________________

❑ Is this Justice the Chief Justice or Associate Justice? Where are they from?

________________________________________

________________________________________

________________________________________

________________________________________

❑ What trials/laws has this Justice been part of?

Do you agree with how they voted?

________________________________________

________________________________________

________________________________________

________________________________________

❑ When voting for a Presidential candidate – do you consider their choice of Justice Candidates?

________________________________________

________________________________________

________________________________________

# U.S. Justice ___________________________

❑ What President nominated this Justice? How many Presidents, have they served under?

______________________________________________

______________________________________________

______________________________________________

______________________________________________

______________________________________________

❑ Is this Justice the Chief Justice or Associate Justice? Where are they from?

______________________________________________

______________________________________________

______________________________________________

______________________________________________

______________________________________________

❑ What trials/laws has this Justice been part of?

Do you agree with how they voted?

______________________________________________

______________________________________________

______________________________________________

______________________________________________

❑ When voting for a Presidential candidate – do you consider their choice of Justice Candidates?

______________________________________________

______________________________________________

______________________________________________

## U.S. Justice _______________________

❏ What President nominated this Justice? How many Presidents, have they served under?

_______________________________________

_______________________________________

_______________________________________

_______________________________________

_______________________________________

❏ Is this Justice the Chief Justice or Associate Justice? Where are they from?

_______________________________________

_______________________________________

_______________________________________

_______________________________________

_______________________________________

❏ What trials/laws has this Justice been part of?

Do you agree with how they voted?

_______________________________________

_______________________________________

_______________________________________

_______________________________________

❏ When voting for a Presidential candidate – do you consider their choice of Justice Candidates?

_______________________________________

_______________________________________

_______________________________________

_______________________________________

## U.S. Justice  _______________________________

❑ What President nominated this Justice? How many
   Presidents, have they served under?

_______________________________________________

_______________________________________________

_______________________________________________

_______________________________________________

_______________________________________________

❑ Is this Justice the Chief Justice or Associate Justice?
   Where are they from?

_______________________________________________

_______________________________________________

_______________________________________________

_______________________________________________

_______________________________________________

❑ What trials/laws has this Justice been part of?

Do you agree with how they voted?

_______________________________________________

_______________________________________________

_______________________________________________

_______________________________________________

_______________________________________________

❑ When voting for a Presidential candidate – do you
   consider their choice of Justice Candidates?

_______________________________________________

_______________________________________________

_______________________________________________

_______________________________________________

# U.S. Justice  ______________________________

❑ What President nominated this Justice? How many
  Presidents, have they served under?

  ______________________________________________

  ______________________________________________

  ______________________________________________

  ______________________________________________

  ______________________________________________

❑ Is this Justice the Chief Justice or Associate Justice?
  Where are they from?

  ______________________________________________

  ______________________________________________

  ______________________________________________

  ______________________________________________

  ______________________________________________

❑ What trials/laws has this Justice been part of?

Do you agree with how they voted?

  ______________________________________________

  ______________________________________________

  ______________________________________________

  ______________________________________________

  ______________________________________________

❑ When voting for a Presidential candidate – do you
  consider their choice of Justice Candidates?

  ______________________________________________

  ______________________________________________

  ______________________________________________

# U.S. Justice _________________________

❏ What President nominated this Justice? How many Presidents, have they served under?

❏ Is this Justice the Chief Justice or Associate Justice? Where are they from?

❏ What trials/laws has this Justice been part of?

Do you agree with how they voted?

❏ When voting for a Presidential candidate – do you consider their choice of Justice Candidates?

# U.S. Justice _______________________

❑ What President nominated this Justice? How many
  Presidents, have they served under?

_______________________________________

_______________________________________

_______________________________________

_______________________________________

_______________________________________

❑ Is this Justice the Chief Justice or Associate Justice?
  Where are they from?

_______________________________________

_______________________________________

_______________________________________

_______________________________________

_______________________________________

❑ What trials/laws has this Justice been part of?

Do you agree with how they voted?

_______________________________________

_______________________________________

_______________________________________

_______________________________________

_______________________________________

❑ When voting for a Presidential candidate  – do you
  consider their choice of Justice Candidates?

_______________________________________

_______________________________________

_______________________________________

_______________________________________

# U.S. Justice _______________________

❑ What President nominated this Justice? How many Presidents, have they served under?

_______________________________________

_______________________________________

_______________________________________

_______________________________________

_______________________________________

❑ Is this Justice the Chief Justice or Associate Justice? Where are they from?

_______________________________________

_______________________________________

_______________________________________

_______________________________________

_______________________________________

❑ What trials/laws has this Justice been part of?

Do you agree with how they voted?

_______________________________________

_______________________________________

_______________________________________

_______________________________________

❑ When voting for a Presidential candidate – do you consider their choice of Justice Candidates?

_______________________________________

_______________________________________

_______________________________________

_______________________________________

# U.S. Justice ______________________

❑ What President nominated this Justice? How many
   Presidents, have they served under?

______________________________________

______________________________________

______________________________________

______________________________________

❑ Is this Justice the Chief Justice or Associate Justice?
   Where are they from?

______________________________________

______________________________________

______________________________________

______________________________________

❑ What trials/laws has this Justice been part of?

Do you agree with how they voted?

______________________________________

______________________________________

______________________________________

______________________________________

❑ When voting for a Presidential candidate  – do you
   consider their choice of Justice Candidates?

______________________________________

______________________________________

______________________________________

______________________________________

# Finding your Ideal Political Party

In this section – there will be a brief outline as to what each party stands for; what makes them different from one another.

The layout of questions for each party – will help you find, discover, and/or reaffirm your party.

The two major parties – that make our democracy are the Republican Party and the Democratic Party. Along with Independent Parties.

Use the following section; to find what best suits you.

# The Republican Party – GOP (Grand Old Party)

The Republican Party – also known as the GOP; is one of the largest parties in the U.S. – along with the Democratic Party.  The official symbol, of the party is the elephant. Representing color is red.

Republicans are considered to be "conservative" – upholding traditional morals in family, religion, and government. The GOP is based on family values – of things like traditional marriage (heterosexual) between male and female. Christian beliefs in faith and scriptural practices. In government, Republicans believe in "less government interference" – thus leaving individuals to live with minimum government assistance, as possible.

Use this section, by answering the questions – figure out if this party is for you.

Date:_______________________

❑ Would you consider yourself, a conservative?
   Why do you believe that? List the reasons.

_______________________________________

_______________________________________

_______________________________________

_______________________________________

_______________________________________

❑ Are you for heterosexual marriage? Do you
   support family values?

_______________________________________

_______________________________________

_______________________________________

_______________________________________

_______________________________________

❑ Do you see it fit to have religion, mainly
   Christianity – influenced in our government?

_______________________________________

_______________________________________

_______________________________________

_______________________________________

_______________________________________

❑ When you vote, in any election – do you match
   which candidate shares your same values?

_______________________________________

_______________________________________

_______________________________________

_______________________________________

Date:_______________________

❑ Do you feel, the need of less government
involvement, as possible?

___________________________________

___________________________________

___________________________________

___________________________________

___________________________________

❑ Do you believe, every citizen should pay medical
bills, education tuition, and other fees all on their
own?

___________________________________

___________________________________

___________________________________

___________________________________

___________________________________

❑ What are your views on Medicaid, should
congress continue to assist families?

___________________________________

___________________________________

___________________________________

___________________________________

___________________________________

❑ Should the GOP repeal, The Affordable
HealthCare Act?

___________________________________

___________________________________

___________________________________

___________________________________

Date:_______________________

❑ Do you believe Republicans, need to make efforts - to pay down our national debt?

___________________________________
___________________________________
___________________________________
___________________________________
___________________________________

❑ What are your thoughts on protecting our allies, such as the State of Israel?

___________________________________
___________________________________
___________________________________
___________________________________
___________________________________

❑ What are your views on foreign policy? Do you believe we need strong immigration borders?

___________________________________
___________________________________
___________________________________
___________________________________
___________________________________

❑ Do you support DACA? Should the GOP – support or enforce immigration law; of becoming a legal residency?

___________________________________
___________________________________
___________________________________
___________________________________

❑    Republican, check box for yes.

If you checked the box, for a yes on being a Republican; make a list of a GOP President, Senator, and Representative. And research their work.

GOP President: _______________________________

GOP Senator: _______________________________

GOP Rep.: _______________________________

# The Democratic Party

The Democratic Party  - is one of the largest parties, along side with the Republicans. The official symbol, of the party is the donkey. Representing color is blue.

Democrats – are viewed as "liberals"- individuals in support of many views and ideas. Having an open mind to others ways of running our government. This party is in support of things like government assistance, same-sex marriage, and co-existing, by excepting all religions; and relying on current/relevant norms in personal philosophy.

Use this section, by answering the questions – figure out if this party is for you.

Date:__________________

❑ Would you consider yourself a liberal? Are you open to more than one view? List your reasons.

____________________________________

____________________________________

____________________________________

____________________________________

____________________________________

❑ Do you support all types of marriage? Traditional or not? Why?

____________________________________

____________________________________

____________________________________

____________________________________

____________________________________

❑ Do you find it necessary – to have religious influence, in government? Or stay neutral?

____________________________________

____________________________________

____________________________________

____________________________________

____________________________________

❑ When you vote, in any election – do you match which candidate shares your same values?

____________________________________

____________________________________

____________________________________

____________________________________

Date:_______________________

❑ Do you believe, that our government should be
   more involved in our lives?

_______________________________________________

_______________________________________________

_______________________________________________

_______________________________________________

_______________________________________________

❑ Do believe that the government should help – in
   time of need? To taxpayers?

_______________________________________________

_______________________________________________

_______________________________________________

_______________________________________________

_______________________________________________

❑ Do you agree with the motion – that healthcare
   should be a right to every citizen?

_______________________________________________

_______________________________________________

_______________________________________________

_______________________________________________

_______________________________________________

❑ Do you think the Medicaid system/Welfare
   system is needed?

_______________________________________________

_______________________________________________

_______________________________________________

_______________________________________________

Date:_________________________

❑ Some Democrats, believe in tuition-free colleges/universities', do you agree?

_______________________________________

_______________________________________

_______________________________________

_______________________________________

❑ Do you support Planned Parenthood? Do you believe, parents have this right?

_______________________________________

_______________________________________

_______________________________________

_______________________________________

❑ Do you believe in pursuing diplomatic solutions; in the middle east? Why?

_______________________________________

_______________________________________

_______________________________________

_______________________________________

❑ Do you think Congress should fight, to keep DACA – and it's recipients (dreamers) running?

_______________________________________

_______________________________________

_______________________________________

_______________________________________

❏  Democrat, check box for yes.

If you checked the box, for a yes on being a Democrat; make a list of a Democrat President, Senator, and Representative. And research their work.

Dem. President:_______________________________

Dem. Senator: _______________________________

Dem. Rep.:_______________________________

# The Independent American Party

The Independent American Party – is made up of individuals; who are not identified as Republican or Democrat. This party will use the U.S. Colonies Flag; as its symbol. Representing colors are yellow, red, white, and blue. This is one party (of many) to use as an example.

Independents – are viewed as "neutral" or "unbiased" – the party is made up of patriotic citizens; relying on our nation's heritage. This party is not as large as the other parties (mentioned before this section). This party believes in investing in our country – working independently from other nations.

Use this section, by answering the questions – figure out if this party is for you.

Date:_______________________

❑ Are you an Independent? Do you stay neutral, in regards to political agendas/discords?

_______________________________________________

_______________________________________________

_______________________________________________

_______________________________________________

❑ Do you feel – that we can get too caught-up in politics, and distracted from more important issues?

_______________________________________________

_______________________________________________

_______________________________________________

_______________________________________________

❑ Are you able to see the strengths, of the Republicans? List a few.

_______________________________________________

_______________________________________________

_______________________________________________

_______________________________________________

❑ Are you able to see the strengths, of the Democrats? List a few.

_______________________________________________

_______________________________________________

_______________________________________________

_______________________________________________

Date:_______________________

❑ What should Republicans work on? List a few short-comings.

_______________________________________________

_______________________________________________

_______________________________________________

_______________________________________________

_______________________________________________

❑ What should Democrats work on? List a few short-comings.

_______________________________________________

_______________________________________________

_______________________________________________

_______________________________________________

_______________________________________________

❑ What are your views on family? Should this be based on individuals; and not discussed in congress?

_______________________________________________

_______________________________________________

_______________________________________________

_______________________________________________

_______________________________________________

❑ Do you feel, congress is wasting time – because of "politics".

_______________________________________________

_______________________________________________

_______________________________________________

_______________________________________________

Date:________________

❑ Should we live by what our founding fathers
  believed?

_______________________________________

_______________________________________

_______________________________________

_______________________________________

❑ Do you pick a side, by flipping a coin, Red or Blue?
  Or do you choose the best candidate, that fits you?

_______________________________________

_______________________________________

_______________________________________

_______________________________________

❑ Should the U.S. break away from the U.N.? Why
  should we?

_______________________________________

_______________________________________

_______________________________________

_______________________________________

❑ Do you know all the Independent Parties,

in the U.S.?

_______________________________________

_______________________________________

_______________________________________

_______________________________________

❏   Independent, check box for yes.

If you checked the box, for a yes on being an Independent; make a list of an Independent President, Senator, and Representative. And research their work.

Ind. President: ______________________________

Ind. Senator: ______________________________

Ind. Rep.: ______________________________

# Taking Action – Getting Involved

It's highly important to get involved. Once you find what party; you choose to be in – you can then find your morals and standards and pursue them. Your elected officials in your party, need your support.

In this section, you'll have a list of questions that can help you – to stay in-the-loop in local, state, and national rallies/campaigns.

Local:________________________________ Date:__________

❑ Where did this event take place? In your
community, city, or county? Was this a rally, for a
local official?

_______________________________________________

_______________________________________________

_______________________________________________

_______________________________________________

❑ How were you part of it? Did you help pass out
flyers, brochures, pins, etc.?

_______________________________________________

_______________________________________________

_______________________________________________

_______________________________________________

❑ Was there a walk-a-thon, coffee table talk, with
the official?

_______________________________________________

_______________________________________________

_______________________________________________

_______________________________________________

❑Did you support, the party at its headquarters? Or
were you on the field? Or both?

_______________________________________________

_______________________________________________

_______________________________________________

_______________________________________________

Local:_________________________________ Date:__________

❑ Where did this event take place? In your community, city, or county? Was this a rally, for a local official?

_______________________________________________

_______________________________________________

_______________________________________________

_______________________________________________

❑ How were you part of it? Did you help pass out flyers, brochures, pins, etc.?

_______________________________________________

_______________________________________________

_______________________________________________

_______________________________________________

❑ Was there a walk-a-thon, coffee table talk, with the official?

_______________________________________________

_______________________________________________

_______________________________________________

_______________________________________________

❑ Did you support, the party at its headquarters? Or were you on the field? Or both?

_______________________________________________

_______________________________________________

_______________________________________________

_______________________________________________

Local:_______________________________ Date:__________

❑ Where did this event take place? In your
community, city, or county? Was this a rally, for a
local official?
_______________________________________________
_______________________________________________
_______________________________________________
_______________________________________________

❑ How were you part of it? Did you help pass out
flyers, brochures, pins, etc.?

_______________________________________________
_______________________________________________
_______________________________________________
_______________________________________________

❑ Was there a walk-a-thon, coffee table talk, with
the official?

_______________________________________________
_______________________________________________
_______________________________________________
_______________________________________________

❑Did you support, the party at its headquarters? Or
were you on the field? Or both?

_______________________________________________
_______________________________________________
_______________________________________________
_______________________________________________

State:_________________________________ Date:__________

❑ Where did this event take place? In your city,
county, state? Was this a rally, for a state official?

_______________________________________________

_______________________________________________

_______________________________________________

_______________________________________________

❑ How were you part of it? Did you help pass out
flyers, brochures, pins, etc.? Take to social media?

_______________________________________________

_______________________________________________

_______________________________________________

_______________________________________________

❑ Was there a walk-a-thon, coffee table talk, with
the official? Rally campaigns in different cities, in
the state?

_______________________________________________

_______________________________________________

_______________________________________________

_______________________________________________

❑ Did you support, the party at its headquarters? Or
were you on the field? Or both?

_______________________________________________

_______________________________________________

_______________________________________________

_______________________________________________

State:_______________________________ Date:__________

❑ Where did this event take place? In your city,
   county, state? Was this a rally, for a state official?

___________________________________________

___________________________________________

___________________________________________

___________________________________________

___________________________________________

❑ How were you part of it? Did you help pass out
   flyers, brochures, pins, etc.? Take to social media?

___________________________________________

___________________________________________

___________________________________________

___________________________________________

___________________________________________

❑ Was there a walk-a-thon, coffee table talk, with
   the official? Rally campaigns in different cities, in
   the state?

___________________________________________

___________________________________________

___________________________________________

___________________________________________

___________________________________________

❑ Did you support, the party at its headquarters? Or
   were you on the field? Or both?

___________________________________________

___________________________________________

___________________________________________

___________________________________________

State:______________________________ Date:__________

❏ Where did this event take place? In your city, county, state? Was this a rally, for a state official?

_______________________________________________

_______________________________________________

_______________________________________________

_______________________________________________

❏ How were you part of it? Did you help pass out flyers, brochures, pins, etc.? Take to social media?

_______________________________________________

_______________________________________________

_______________________________________________

_______________________________________________

❏ Was there a walk-a-thon, coffee table talk, with the official? Rally campaigns in different cities, in the state?

_______________________________________________

_______________________________________________

_______________________________________________

_______________________________________________

❏ Did you support, the party at its headquarters? Or were you on the field? Or both?

_______________________________________________

_______________________________________________

_______________________________________________

_______________________________________________

National:________________________ Date:________

❑ Where did this event take place? In your state,
  region, or in a far state? What position was this for?

__________________________________________________

__________________________________________________

__________________________________________________

__________________________________________________

__________________________________________________

❑ How were you part of it? Did you help pass out
  flyers, brochures, pins, etc.? Take to social media?

__________________________________________________

__________________________________________________

__________________________________________________

__________________________________________________

__________________________________________________

❑ Were you able to attend a rally? Did you have the
  opportunity to help?

__________________________________________________

__________________________________________________

__________________________________________________

__________________________________________________

__________________________________________________

❑ Did you use social media? Sharing the official's
  page – sharing where the official is going/their
  work?

__________________________________________________

__________________________________________________

__________________________________________________

__________________________________________________

National:_________________________________ Date:_________

❑ Where did this event take place? In your state, region, or in a far state? What position was this for?

_______________________________________________

_______________________________________________

_______________________________________________

_______________________________________________

_______________________________________________

❑ How were you part of it? Did you help pass out flyers, brochures, pins, etc.? Take to social media?

_______________________________________________

_______________________________________________

_______________________________________________

_______________________________________________

_______________________________________________

❑ Were you able to attend a rally? Did you have the opportunity to help?

_______________________________________________

_______________________________________________

_______________________________________________

_______________________________________________

_______________________________________________

❑ Did you use social media? Sharing the official's page – sharing where the official is going/their work?

_______________________________________________

_______________________________________________

_______________________________________________

_______________________________________________

National:_________________________ Date:_______

❑ Where did this event take place? In your state, region, or in a far state? What position was this for?

_______________________________________________

_______________________________________________

_______________________________________________

_______________________________________________

_______________________________________________

❑ How were you part of it? Did you help pass out flyers, brochures, pins, etc.? Take to social media?

_______________________________________________

_______________________________________________

_______________________________________________

_______________________________________________

_______________________________________________

❑ Were you able to attend a rally? Did you have the opportunity to help?

_______________________________________________

_______________________________________________

_______________________________________________

_______________________________________________

_______________________________________________

❑ Did you use social media? Sharing the official's page – sharing where the official is going/their work?

_______________________________________________

_______________________________________________

_______________________________________________

_______________________________________________

# Paying it Forward

U.S. Politics is part of our democracy – and what makes our democracy work; is concerned constituents, like yourself, taking action – standing for what we so passionately believe in. Our government is meant to serve "we the people".

We may not always agree (on many things) however – we all should be grateful. Even though we may be at political odds/oppositions – we are still the land of the free and home of the brave. We are the greatest nation on earth.

Let this section assist you – to pay it forward!

Date:_______________________

❑ Whether you are a Conservative, Liberal, or Independent – are you grateful for our democracy?

_______________________________________

_______________________________________

_______________________________________

_______________________________________

❑ Do you agree – that we have a voice (voting) to use; and we are being heard?

_______________________________________

_______________________________________

_______________________________________

_______________________________________

❑Do you believe we should work together? For the greater good?

_______________________________________

_______________________________________

_______________________________________

_______________________________________

❑ How do you plan to work together, with your opposing political side?

_______________________________________

_______________________________________

_______________________________________

_______________________________________

Date:___________________

❑ Do you plan, to get more involved with your community? What can you do?

_______________________________________

_______________________________________

_______________________________________

_______________________________________

❑ Will you inform/educate those around you – with little knowledge about what is happening; in our nation?

_______________________________________

_______________________________________

_______________________________________

_______________________________________

❑ Are you registered to vote? Vote regularly? And encourage others to vote?

_______________________________________

_______________________________________

_______________________________________

_______________________________________

❑ Do you believe that one vote can make a difference? Why?

_______________________________________

_______________________________________

_______________________________________

_______________________________________

Every citizen in the United States of America, is so blessed and fortunate to live in our beloved nation. Our shared liberty and freedom should always serve as a beacon of hope and prosperity, to the rest of the world.

Thank you, for purchasing this journal. Please keep a look out for more; and feel free to leave your review.

Best Wishes,

Daniel A. Garcia